Magical Beasts for Beginners

Maverick

Early Readers

'Magical Beasts for Beginners'
An original concept by Heather Pindar
© Heather Pindar 2023

Illustrated by Letizia Rizzo

Published by MAVERICK ARTS PUBLISHING LTD
Studio 11, City Business Centre, 6 Brighton Road,
Horsham, West Sussex, RH13 5BB
© Maverick Arts Publishing Limited May 2023
+44 (0)1403 256941

A CIP catalogue record for this book is available at the British Library.

ISBN 978-1-84886-961-5

www.maverickbooks.co.uk

This book is rated as: Gold Band (Guided Reading)

Magical Beasts for Beginners

By Heather Pindar

Illustrated by Letizia Rizzo

Chapter 1

Lily-May and her older brother, Gus, were spending Saturday at Grandad's. They loved helping out at his very special animal rescue centre deep in the Scottish Highlands: The Home for Magical Beasts.

Dear Toothy-Grinned Gus and Bright-Eyed Lily-May,

I've gone for a wander. I'll be back at exactly the right time. Please look after the magical beasts. Follow these instructions carefully and all will be well.

Thank you.

Love, Grandad.

"Is this another one of Grandad's jokes?" said Lily-May.

"I don't know," said Gus. "Read his note again."

Grandad had left the note poking out of a large book next to the biscuit tin in the kitchen. Lily-May slowly read out the note to Gus again.

"Hmm. The note sounds a bit strange, but I think Grandad is serious," said Gus. "And his hang glider has gone, so he's definitely not here. He's really left us in charge of the magical beasts!"

"Oooh, exciting!" Lily-May said. "But what about the big book? Do we need the book as well as the instructions?"

Gus looked at the cover of the book. "It's called *Magical Beasts for Beginners*, but we've been helping Grandad look after the magical beasts for years! I already know lots about them. *I'm* not a beginner!"

"But I like this book," said Lily-May. "Look at these beautiful pictures! And all this extra information about the beasts! I'm going to keep it with me, just in case..."

"Whatever!" said Gus.

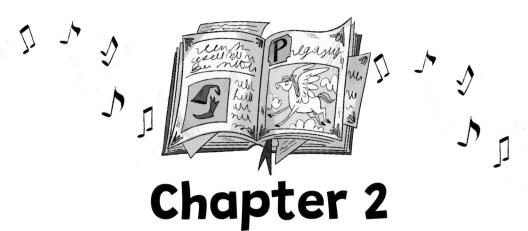

Chapter 2

"Instruction number 1," said Lily-May.

Check the tricksy pixies and the three
young elves,
Are playing nicely and behaving themselves.

"They're probably in here," said Gus,
running up the steps to the tree house.
He peeped inside. "Great! They're all fast
asleep."

"Really?" said Lily-May. "They're usually very lively."

"Yep! Sleeping like babies," said Gus. "That was easy-peasy. What's next?"

"Instruction number 2," said Lily-May, giggling. "It's another of Grandad's funny rhyming ones."

The sniffin' griffin with the scales of gold,
Needs toast and socks to keep out the cold.

"Oh yes!" said Gus, "The griffin is sniffing because she's got a cold. Easy-peasy again! We won't need help from that beginners' book."

Gus and Lily-May checked on the griffin in the barn. She looked cosy, resting on the straw. They ran back to the house to make toast and search for socks.

What they saw when they returned to the barn made them gasp.

The pixies were chasing each other around the barn and swinging like monkeys between the roof beams. The elves were banging on the walls and shrieking with glee.

"They were just pretending to be asleep!" wailed Lily-May.

"I'll sort this," said Gus stepping forward. He held up his hand. "STOP!" he shouted. "Stop that right now!"

The pixies and elves stopped. They stared at Gus. The biggest pixie giggled. Then they all started running about and shrieking again.

"Argh!" said Gus, "*Now* what do we do?"

Chapter 3

"Listen, Gus," said Lily-May. "I looked under 'B' for badly-behaved beasts. It says they'll calm down if you get them to dance the Highland Fling."

"Really?" said Gus, frowning. "That sounds ridiculous."

"Well, I believe in the book and I'm going to try it," said Lily-May.

Lily-May had learnt the Highland Fling
at school. She began the dance: hopping,
jumping and turning.

At first, the pixies and elves ignored
Lily-May. But one by one, they began to join
in with the dance. Gus stared in amazement.

"Keep going, Lily-May!" he said. "It's like
you put a spell on them."

Lily-May began to dance out of the door. The pixies and elves followed her back to the tree house steps.

"Up you go," said Lily-May. "Play nicely and stay out of the barn."

Gus made more toast and Lily-May gently pulled the socks up the griffin's legs.

"*Now* do you believe in the book?" she asked.

"Maybe," muttered Gus.

"ACHOO!" said the griffin.

"Yuck!" said Lily-May, wiping the green gunk off her neck.

Chapter 4

"Instruction number 3," said Gus.

Bring the beasts snacks and tea around half past three,
But don't give spaghetti to the wild-eyed yeti.

"That's easy," added Gus. "I'll make the tea; you sort out the snacks."

"Give spaghetti to the wild-eyed yeti? No problem," said Lily-May. "There's a bowlful right here."

"No, *don't* give spaghetti to the wild-eyed yeti," said Gus.

But Lily-May didn't hear him.

"MMMM SPAGHETTI!" slurped the wild-eyed yeti, as she put the bowl in front of him. The yeti tipped all the spaghetti into his mouth.

"You didn't give the wild-eyed yeti spaghetti, did you?" asked Gus.

"Yes!" said Lily-May. "And he wants more!"

The yeti jumped through the open window.

"Uh-oh," said Gus.

"Stop, yeti!" yelled Lily-May. But the yeti was already running down the hill, sniffing the air for more spaghetti.

Chapter 5

Gus's phone beeped.

"It's a text from Grandad!"

If things go wrong,
Play the Wild Water Song.

"I'll check the book!" said Lily-May. "Yes!
It's here, under 'W'. It says the Wild Water
Song will call the monster from the loch* to
come and help!"

*Loch is the Scots, Scottish Gaelic and Irish word for a lake.

"Really? Amazing!" said Gus. He peered at the page. "I think I can play this song. Grandad's been teaching me the bagpipes."

"I know!" said Lily-May. "I heard you practising."

When Gus started to play, Lily-May felt a shiver run up her back. The notes of the beautiful Wild Water Song rang out perfectly to the end.

BOOM! BOOM! BOOM!

"The monster's here!" said Lily-May. "And she's got the wild-eyed yeti!"

The yeti was sitting on the monster's back. He waved happily at Gus and Lily-May.

"I can't believe it," said Lily-May. "The wild-eyed yeti loves his monster ride. He's forgotten all about the spaghetti."

"Shhh! Don't mention the spaghetti," whispered Gus.

Chapter 6

"Thank you," said Lily-May, looking up at the monster. "What's next, Gus?"

"Nothing!" said Gus. "We've done everything on Grandad's list!"

"Hurray! Grandad will be impressed," said Lily-May. "We'd better get the yeti back inside... Oh no! What are those troublemakers doing out here?"

The pixies and elves were on the large patch of grass in front of Grandad's house. They started a noisy game of tag.

Gus and Lily-May heard a loud 'Hello there!' above them.

"Look! It's Grandad!" said Gus. "He can't land – the pixies and elves are in his way."

Grandad steered wildly to the left.
The glider swerved sharply and crashed into the branches of a huge pine tree.

"Help!" called Grandad. "I'm stuck!"

The loch monster roared. She turned and poked her head into the tree where Grandad was stuck. Grandad climbed awkwardly onto her neck. He slid down with a loud 'Woo-hoo!'

The yeti stumbled forwards and caught Grandad clumsily.

"Och, that was great! Thank you!" he said, smiling up at the yeti and the monster.

BOOM! BOOM! BOOM!

The monster swam away across the loch.

"You've both done very well indeed," said Grandad. "And you're still just beginners so I'm even more impressed!"

"We couldn't have done it without the book," said Gus.

"And soon we won't be beginners anymore," said Lily-May.

"Well, I was a beginner until I was 23," said Grandpa with a smile, "and I'm 76 now and I'm still learning. Now follow me, there's someone I want you to meet."

Grandad led Gus and Lily-May to one of the stables. "She's not lost, or injured, and she'll always be here when you come to visit."

"A Highland pony... for us? Thanks, Grandad!" said Gus. Lily-May flung her arms around the pony's neck.

"Instruction number 4," said Grandad, winking at Gus. "Think of a name for your hairy orange pony... But whatever you do, don't feed her macaroni."

Lily-May looked at Gus and they burst out laughing.

The End

Book Bands for Guided Reading

The Institute of Education book banding system is a scale of colours that reflects the various levels of reading difficulty. The bands are assigned by taking into account the content, the language style, the layout and phonics. Word, phrase and sentence level work is also taken into consideration.

Maverick Early Readers are a bright, attractive range of books covering the pink to white bands. All of these books have been book banded for guided reading to the industry standard and edited by a leading educational consultant.

Pink

Red

Yellow

Blue

Green

Orange

Turquoise

Purple

Gold

White

To view the whole Maverick Readers scheme, visit our website at
www.maverickearlyreaders.com

Or scan the QR code above to view our scheme instantly!